READY TO ANSWER WITH HUNGER

STACY BOE MILLER

POETRY

Printed in the United States of America

First Edition
1 2 3 4 5 6 7 8 9

Cover image To be good by Wynter Jones

ISBN 978-1-949540-60-4

C&R Press
crpress.org

Praise for
Ready to Answer with Hunger

"These are poems of Wyoming and girlhood and shiny boots and a God who 'was good / for lots of things,' as you've never heard them before: full of 'all the tangle / and wild' of queer desire, of exorcisms, of motherhood and children who 'bit off the tongues / of their mothers,' and of ghost fathers with their arms full of antiques. When Stacy Boe Miller writes, 'I want you to live here / with me. Maybe you already do. I guess I want you to say it,' I am overjoyed to answer yes. These are full-hearted, full-voiced, necessary poems that are gritty and funny and fearless in what they both ask and offer. I'm so grateful we all get to live awhile in and with her voice."
-Alexandra Teague, author of *[ominous music intensifying]*

"The power of *Ready to Answer with Hunger* is its firm refusal to erect social, poetic, and personal divisions between joy, sorrow, lust, guilt, violence, daily pleasure, deep intimacy, or considerations of the sacred. Everything in Stacy Boe Miller's world is seen and attested to with nuance and meaning, from suicide and religious extremism to the most common and meaningful acts a day might bring, whether that's combing a child's hair or throwing on a set of snow chains in a neglected corner of America. The poems here are built from materials that last, and we have before us a new and thrilling voice."
-Michael McGriff, author of *Inquest* and *Angel Sharpening its Beak*

"An essential wisdom lives in Auden's quip, that poetry is 'the clear expression of mixed feelings.' It is wisdom in regards to poetry but to life as well: we want what we want even when we don't have a clear idea what it is we desire. Stacy Boe Miller's poems are a life's story about that place, that nexus, the self in a world of abundance and deprivation, despair and joy, fulfillment and vacancy. *Ready to Answer with Hunger* is not a map but a landscape spread out before us, full of mountains, birds, and rivers, and it's walked by a woman who has spent a life wondering 'what we were hoping for,' and almost believing there's 'a line we would draw if we had any / power to draw that kind of line.' It's a walk you should take with her, full of histories, beauties, and revelations. Stacy Boe Miller has that power."
-Robert Wrigley

Praise for
Ready to Answer with Hunger

"These are poems of Wyoming and girlhood and shiny boots and a God who 'was good / for lots of things,' as you've never heard them before: full of 'all the tangle / and wild' of queer desire, of exorcisms, of motherhood and children who 'bit off the tongues / of their mothers,' and of ghost fathers with their arms full of antiques. When Stacy Boe Miller writes, 'I want you to live here / with me. Maybe you already do. I guess I want you to say it,' I am overjoyed to answer yes. These are full-hearted, full-voiced, necessary poems that are gritty and funny and fearless in what they both ask and offer. I'm so grateful we all get to live awhile in and with her voice."
-Alexandra Teague, author of *[ominous music intensifying]*

"The power of *Ready to Answer with Hunger* is its firm refusal to erect social, poetic, and personal divisions between joy, sorrow, lust, guilt, violence, daily pleasure, deep intimacy, or considerations of the sacred. Everything in Stacy Boe Miller's world is seen and attested to with nuance and meaning, from suicide and religious extremism to the most common and meaningful acts a day might bring, whether that's combing a child's hair or throwing on a set of snow chains in a neglected corner of America. The poems here are built from materials that last, and we have before us a new and thrilling voice."
-Michael McGriff, author of *Inquest* and *Angel Sharpening its Beak*

"An essential wisdom lives in Auden's quip, that poetry is 'the clear expression of mixed feelings.' It is wisdom in regards to poetry but to life as well: we want what we want even when we don't have a clear idea what it is we desire. Stacy Boe Miller's poems are a life's story about that place, that nexus, the self in a world of abundance and deprivation, despair and joy, fulfillment and vacancy. *Ready to Answer with Hunger* is not a map but a landscape spread out before us, full of mountains, birds, and rivers, and it's walked by a woman who has spent a life wondering 'what we were hoping for,' and almost believing there's 'a line we would draw if we had any / power to draw that kind of line.' It's a walk you should take with her, full of histories, beauties, and revelations. Stacy Boe Miller has that power."
-Robert Wrigley

READY TO ANSWER WITH HUNGER

for my father

TABLE OF CONTENTS

I

I

Hypothetical

Let's say a kid goes to church camp
every summer, sometimes
sleeps on the top bunk, and some
summers lifts her hands while singing,
feels her fingers tingle
and knows there's a big beyond.

Say sometimes the room becomes a river,
and this kid gets swept away. Maybe
she's a stick in the current
and she's sure one day
this river will flood the whole world.

Maybe it's made of a heavenly language
she can suddenly speak, and that might be proof
she's on the right track.

Say one year the pastor holds up a cup of water,
asks the kids if they would drink
if he put in a drop, only a drop—let's say
he emphasizes that—of sewer water.
Maybe he squeaks a marker across
a whiteboard, *Clean water mixed with dirty water*
equals dirty water. And he's clever
so uses a drop of blue food coloring.

Say this kid is watching close
how those tiny blue tendrils reach
every way, and she's trying
to wrap her hands around a river, keep that holy raging
alive in her mind. And let's just go ahead
and say she wants so badly, more than
anything, to be clean.

In the Tree Fort

My sister gives me a cigarette,
says I don't even have to
inhale. I take in a cloud of
a different world, blow it
back out of my mouth. She doesn't

know she'll soon tear up
her knee, marry a man
it will be smart to fear,
doesn't see herself calling
our father from a gas station
with only her purse and pajamas.

I don't yet feel the pull I will
toward the wrong
kind of love, the demons
my pastor will try to drive out,

or the babies I'll birth, two slipping from me
just slivers of themselves. We watch

my mother across the pasture,
pinning our clothes to the line. She doesn't
look up to see our legs dangle,

our fingers move to our lips,
looking for what the world will offer,
ready to answer with hunger.

Andi and Me, by Bighorn Creek

catching rainbow trout for dinner.
She hands me her pole and I don't
ask, just slide a hook through the body

of a worm. She casts into the sparkle, her face
focused as she jerks and reels. It's big enough
for dinner, big enough to begin

her unfolding in these mountains away
from her father. Around him she folds herself small
as the heart of a trout. I don't mind

cleaning her fish, wiping my hands down
my jeans, the shimmer evidence of something
I can do. Knife prick into soft

belly and up toward the gills like
a line we would draw if we had any
power to draw that kind of line.

Creation Myth of My Father

He cracks his elbows
on his mother's early
death. At the funeral,
adults say, *Stay*
out of the way.

His calves grow stone
hitchhiking gravel. He lights
a driver's cigarette,
and also his long beard.

Blows from bar fights
across his chest. And a woman
latched to his back defending
her boyfriend. His face, boxing-glove
leather. He's skinning a deer. Just one

rodeo. His fingers
and knees—concrete
trucks grind sunrise.

He sets a teenage wife down
among cactus, antelope, and twenty below.

There's a broken baby
who can be fixed for $30,000,
three too early to live, and two outside
putting pennies on the train track.

He's a forest so big, we hide
and seek through him. A map
we check so often,
we never learn

the direction of the trails.
He's a bridge I've crossed
so many times, I don't
know how I'll swim.

I Build an Altar for My Family to Pray

Dad lifts my braid,
twists a tick
from the base of my head.

My fourteen-year-old brother
drives us to the lake, takes
a gravel corner
too fast.

Cancer grows on my mother's face
where she offers
her milky skin to the sun.

I sing into my parents' mirror,
stop short at an angel
through the wooden wall.

Wind blows open
the front door, and our horse
walks into the kitchen.

Our little white car
tumbleweeds the ditch. I wake
in the back seat having dreamed
my first six years.

My grandfather walks
from his garden eating an onion
like an apple.

A preacher tells me
I'll be a martyr—says God
has a special plan.

Don't look under the bandage
we tell my mother, *no matter*
how much you want to.

Dad fries the heart of a deer
he killed. I let it
melt on my tongue.

Our dog runs through the pasture
with a block of government cheese.
Mom thanks the Lord
and makes lunch.

> My sister sprints
> a mile back to the trailer
> while the boys and I stand waiting
> for the car to explode.

My brother on his girlfriend's
porch when something invisible
punches him in the jaw.

Dad hunch-shouldered
away from the phone. Cries
and says cousin Mark
shot himself dead.

> Wyoming brushes my sister's hair
> from her face. Her legs, graveling
> away from us. My brother's eyes—

I sit on my Holly Hobby bedspread
imagining Hell.

> My brother's eyes
> like broken windshields
> watching for wings
> of flame.

Equality State

My boots are still shiny because
I didn't actually ride horses
that much, though once in the Big Horn Mountains
the one beneath me took off
full gallop toward the corral. *Barn sour,*
my cousin's wife said. I know sometimes

we just want to go home. How Chris LeDoux must have felt
when he sang, *Take me back to old Wyoming.*
He had that tall son
I couldn't keep my eyes off
when our basketball teams played.
His long farmer-tan arms. I liked to picture
his ranch chores, the sky barely blushing.
His hair a little too long by the ears, shaggy
under the rim of his hat. That's what people think of
when they think of Wyoming: hats and horses, and now a boy

left broken near a fence. I think of that
boy too, think of Matthew a lot,
how terrifying a long lone fence can be.
And I think of the miners, stripping the overburden
of topsoil late in the night, praying
for their sleeping kids. Kids who might wake up

and decorate a homecoming float with blue and white balloons,
put on football jerseys, thumb dip into their bottom lips,
wave at smiling moms on the sidewalk and hope
to get into their girlfriends' pants after
the game. It works sometimes—

those jerseys, Wranglers with chew-can rings,
hands callused from pull-ups or dirt-bike
work. Western girls go crazy for
that shit, lie down in boys' pickups and dream

themselves onto a little ranch, maybe
in the Big Horns like my Aunt Jean, branding
cattle, baking pies for my leathery Uncle Chuck
who could *whip about anybody,* my dad said, until
that final week when conscience crept up
Chuck's throat like well water. He spent his last three days
calling everyone he'd wronged, begging,

Please forgive me, terrified to meet the Lord
with all that sediment in his soul. *I forgive you,*
my mom said. She's not sure
she meant it, but it was
a kind thing to say.

Mother, Any Given Day

Across two cattle guards,
past the curve of the sewer pond,
my mother puts chains on the tires
of our pickup. Burns garbage
in a metal trash can. Sings
to the piano, *Nothing*
but the Blood of Jesus.
The notes rise

from her fingers like cactus spines
in the pasture I roam. She watches
through the window as she sews
our Easter dresses, thinks of the children

God took home. She knows as well
as that prickly pear how our bodies are
hidden waters. Sometimes she laughs so hard

she cries and we tease her,
but even in my smallness
I know it's a soft rare bloom.
Sometimes she closes

the bathroom door and keeps the crying
quiet. With winter approaching

succulents die back to unseen
things—roots below ground,
bulbs that could never last
in this wide open.

For Cousins

This is Mark on the front porch with a gun
in his mouth. The wind cold and heavy. A meadowlark
is singing. Maybe Mark is singing, *Peace Be Still*, might think
for a second of his brother who sang it

in front of church, off-key.
This is Mark's brother checking cattle in a pasture
nearby, heat from the horse beneath him
steaming the winter air. He doesn't look up
when he hears the shot. It's Wyoming after all. This

is the moment right before knowing. Let's lay it
on the table, fold back the corners, smooth any wrinkles:
A young man turns his horse home, the only sound,

hooves on dirt, and maybe sandhill cranes like we saw
that summer, their legs going on so long beneath them. Or maybe
the sky is empty—there's not a bird for miles.

We Were Mothers

even before we were. Lifting
dirty, pink shirts to cradle
plastic babies to our flat chests.

Feel, we'd say years later
in line for the swings, and squeeze
each other's small, sore breasts.
Womanhood hidden but surely there

like the things Lorna said
our parents did in their bedrooms.
Sometimes we'd hold crayons
between our fingers, take drags,

blow up and away from their little faces
like we'd seen
the good moms do.

The Sign on the Highway Reads, "Best Town on Earth"

There's a boy in a cage
in a basement. Downtown
everyone is coffee shopping
or learning to change
their bicycle tires. A class field trip
at the museum for red onions.
A prom queen in a dress
made of Cool Ranch Dorito bags.
We need more staples for all
these plastic flowers. I try to walk
like my sister, feet turned out,
down the sidewalk to the only
drug store. Tonight, I will
slice my forearm on the fence
of the public pool, and jump in
anyway, for the feeling
of being swallowed. Above,
moths break their bodies.
It's not self-sacrifice—
they just want to be the light.

God Was Always Talking

Kip, he said, *throw your records*
in the lake. Now walk barefoot
toward the world and tell everyone

I'm your favorite. Down by the dock he whispered
to Karen, *Those birds in the sky—*
are just birds. We passed that story around.

He told my sister to quit
college, hurry up and marry
the wrong man. He told
Eric to break my heart
and announce it to the whole
group. Folks were told to

cut their hair, buy a new bathing suit,
split up or finally hold hands. He told Fran
to buy that BMW, but we judged her
anyway. God was good

for lots of things. He handed
Greg Miller a shiny ring and his wife
a brand-new keyboard. Connie received a divine
Gatorade bottle that never went dry
even in Atlanta heat. Amanda got angels

for taxi drivers, prophetic
dreams, seven children. He gave me a safety pin
once, stuck in the leaf of a plant, and I mended
my broken sandal. My brother asked

for a weight set, wrote it on a piece of paper
I tucked into the Wailing Wall. Jim was trusting
God for a root canal. And Jared gave all

his money to visiting missionaries, covered
his fuel gauge with a sticky note. One Israel-loving
prophet said God

was going to give me that new car
I was believing Him for, and suddenly
I wanted a new car.

After Dark

We snuck to our yards
to peer in windows
at our own mothers
readying themselves
for the night, slipping rings off
into small bowls by their beds,
pumping lotion into palms
and wringing their fingers over
and over around soft hands. They pulled

pins from tight up-dos, and shook
their heads. Reaching into some secret
place, a small latch below
the left breast, a hidden button
between pinky and ring finger,
tiny lock behind an ear, they pried
open doors only they knew.
We watched our mothers
draw from these small caves

the birds that live inside—songbirds,
or magpies, sandpipers, crows.
They stroked feathers,
or spoke gently. Some smiled.
Then all would
tuck those creatures
back into the dark. We closed

our eyes and breathed in
the night smell. We laid hands on
our chests, wrists, ears,
and wondered

what—if ever that kind of thing
were allowed—the birds
of our mothers would sing.

My Church Called Their Exorcism Program *Healing House*

Oh you're a tough one, my pastor's wife laughed
when the demon inside me screamed
Fuck you! I blamed Eve—

that bitch—who could have eaten from
any other tree. She curled inside me
like a tapeworm, woke me with a hunger

parade in my throat. How
did I feel when I kissed
a woman? My pastor told me to

name it   pull it away from my chest. Shame
stitched the truth to the tender pink
of my gums so I whispered only *Filthy.*

My mother used a seam ripper when she sewed
mistakes. In the bright of her room, tearing
threads. I am still tugging at the way

I should have answered.   That is to say,
when I kissed her we shivered as if we were
cold, but we weren't, and we were brave

so we didn't close our eyes. I held
my breath all day. I might still be holding
my breath.   That is to say   kissing her

made me feel like water
must feel when a well is finally dug,
when all that buried shimmer

witches its way to the surface, when
from under famined clay, something,
dear god   reveals itself as life.

I Want to Wreck This

We met in the middle
of setting our own
traps. I asked you to put your mouth

on my mouth, and you
did. How do you say
stay to someone no longer

here? How do you touch
when you can't find your
own hands? Inside my body, feathers

fester between ribs. Inside
my body, grandmas
eat my stories. When you call,
I smile, don't tell you

I'm frightened by the magpies
in my yard. *We could never
be together,* you say. Inside my body,
a house is burning down.

Boil Down

Dirtied rivers circling
my mouth, bird bones under
my bed. I abused the neighbor's
dog once, just for a moment. Who's in
charge now? Filled
with the Holy Spirit. A stranger
on a bus reaching around
the stranger between us, his hand on
the back of my neck. Campfire
in my lungs, mothball in
my mouth. The scar
on my back numb
in the worst way. An older boy holding me
down, dropping bits of chewed apple
in my mouth. Collapsed-weeping
in the clean shower water
again. What's another word
for weeping? A robin bashing her body
against my window. Your finger
on my lips in the Sunday
School room. Blood seeping
through my light green jeans. Jesus
on the wall of our church, hungry
as the deer too weak to carry herself off
Snow Road. My family following
in the van slowly, slowly, no one
saying a word.

An Altar in the World

I pick up a stone and name it
Every time you've hurt me. I keep it

in my mouth, let it click
against my teeth. The feather tangled

in my hair is from a country
called *Your father's dying.* Someday

I will be enough feather and tangle
to lift myself away. The hawk-scream

through my window is *My grandfather
used to pray for me.* Holy oil

from a jar inside his shirt pocket
rides the currents of my skin. Some

things have no names yet: the pine arrow,
the robin's beak, the washer

I wear on a string that could
break any moment.

Playground

Sometimes, sharp teeth children
bite off the tongues
of their mothers. The world is
filled with their smacking. Words

shaped around a pulpy mess.
Pigtail girl kicking herself
back and forth on the swing,
dump truck boy, costume bin
children, firefighters, princesses,
crawling through the yawn

at the top of the slide, all mouthing,
like a peach pit or hard candy,
their mothers' throbbing
tongues. And the mothers

run the curve of the merry-
go-round, move toward muffled
calls of *Underdog!* wipe dripping
noses, bend to tie laces, while
the orchid of their silence
is opening.

The Audience

thinks I look lovely
when I sleep, was furious

when you said I need to lose weight.
Stores sold out of tissue when I lost

my baby. I'm careful
to chew with my mouth closed. I stare

out windows sometimes, rake
my fingers through my hair, maybe brush

them down my chest. I feel so sexy,
they can tell. When I'm running,

a song comes on I know
they can hear. It's dramatic—

the music, my steadfast
look. They lean

forward. We are all thinking of
my marriage, the wings I almost

grew. We remember my tears in the shower
until the water ran cold and I shivered

on the dirty, orange floor. They are really on my side
now. Some are crying and their chests

begin to hurt. The beat keeps banging
into them and I'm running so fast.

Miscarriage

Was wolves
took the baby
into the throat of
the woods. She'll be cold

sometimes, but she won't know
the shame of her body. You may
see her years from now, among

the cedars. Isn't it beautiful
how she doesn't cover herself
with her hands? You'll look

out the window and imagine
her teeth—sharp
enough for flesh, blackening

feet below her ankles. You'll dream her
hair filled with branches.
It could make you

jealous, all the tangle
and wild. You'll stand in the yard
some nights, try to
trade your voice for howl.

What to Do with the Hate You've Been Hauling

Grind it in your Cuisinart. Pulse
to a fine powder.
Push it into capsules
to urge down your throat
past the swamp of your belly

deep into your hip sockets or under
your kneecap moon. Circle
it round the fire wick
at the base of your skull.

Mix it with coconut oil
and rub it into your thirsty
skin—extra on the aging décolletage
and summer-season dry heels.

Dry it in the sun, until it crisps
and flakes just right for one clean
push into the ears. Box it in
so all you hear
is its crackling song.

Make a house of it—brick
up the windows and doors. No
chimney for escape in case you
change your mind. You can

dance and sleep and shit
and eat, and no one
will touch you. No one.

With Snow Heavy on Everything

We hold our secrets in. The town
fattens with unspoken
desires. The year
rolls over, and we hope in this one

we'll grow comfortable
with hunger. My brother watches his prayers
turn to fog. My mother watches the clock.

Fistfuls of pure white hair let go of
my father's beautiful head.

Is This What the Yeti Feels?

Bigfoot, or the Loch Ness Monster? Riding
a pathetic teeter-totter of being

myth and fact. Even this aching
can't push it hard right or hard left. Let me

be honest. Middle age sags above me
like a warped ceiling. I am tired

of hearing from young people that I am in fact
cool. *In what part of your body are you feeling*

the sadness? my therapist asks. I lay my hands
across my chest and the burning correctness

makes me cry. An owl keeps waking me, and I lie
in the tempting fear of what it might mean.

I touch my husband's skin and think mostly of the bones
beneath. How long can they last? I miss being sure

about eternity. The words I'm speaking
these days eat up all the words I have

spoken before. Is there no one else in this forest
besides me and my fears—mountaining themselves

so big I can live on them? I want you to live here
with me. Maybe you already do. I guess I want you to say it.

There Now

I have a son with long black hair.
He still asks me sometimes to brush it.

I stand on a stool to make sure
I get the tangles on top.

He has another mother
in a different country. She's young

enough to be my child as well. I take
time with the brushing, some evenings

make three thick ropes and braid
them together. I stare at his shoulders,

the track of his spine. I watch us
in the mirror. He's patient

with me, doesn't talk while I work
through the curls. When I finish

I say, *There*, and like a thief
clutch the brush to my chest.

II

Spring

Branches open tiny fists,
hold them up to
tired faces.

The crack of bat
against ball reaches out to us
on our porch. My children stop

fighting for a moment, notice
a tanager, breathe, *What*
is it? Our half of the world

leans an ear toward the shoulder
of the sun. Inside
my father, an organ whispers,
I don't care
who you think
you are.
I lean my ear toward a body that is barely

my father. I gather
the petals falling

from his story. My hands
are getting so full.

Thoughts from My Time on the Moon

Nothing prepares you for the starkness. —Buzz Aldrin

Craters cast shadows
like, *What might be missing?*
Boulders the size of small cars like,
What might be too much?

When Earth rises, I imagine all the girls

down there standing on scales, plucking
eyebrows, stuffing bras. I can't see from here
my daughter

watching a show about a necessary
makeover. Lifting her shirt

to the mirror, she squeezes the skin of her
beautiful, pale belly.

Mr. Aldrin, I hear you read from Genesis
up here. I didn't have to
bring that book. They carved the story of that hijacked
apple into my brain years ago. And oxygen?

What woman needs it? We've grown
so comfortable holding our breath.

Church

Muzzles gone white on old dogs church,
quadriceps screaming uphill
on gravel bike church, garbanzos dancing
in their dry rattles church, his finger finally
finding your clitoris church, alone
on the toilet birthing
a dead baby church, church of the first time
you kissed a girl, "Twinkle Twinkle Little Star"
fiddled poorly in a park at
night church, tomatoes
ripe in a garden you planted
with your mother church, jukebox
that still takes quarters church,
your father might be dying
church, sleeping with your children in
your blood-stained sheets church,
church of slow dancing
with your son, lying to siblings
church, not knowing it's the last
time you will nurse
a child church, church of finding
an arrowhead and losing it,
being ripped open
by a baby church, church of the lump
in your breast, church of finally loving
your legs, becoming the mother
of another woman's child church, *where*
two or more are gathered in
the best dive bar in Idaho church, *there*
I will be also timing your in-breath
with his out-breath, filling your lungs
with *on this rock I will build*
my church.

It Was the Summer of Hard Tomatoes

sucking into themselves like I shied
inward when asked, *How*
is your father? like my father's shoulders

collapsed toward his ribs.
I rubbed them softly
while mom magneted
Do Not Resuscitate

to the fridge. I learned
to sleep everywhere—plastic
chairs, a bench at the end
of his hospital bed,
even with the fourth of July
outside, or helicopters daily
landing on the roof. I pulled

food into myself with a new
desperation—dark pudding with skin
on top, papery rice noodles,
fresh cherries until
I was sick. In the last days,

his mind went back
to work. He worried about the concrete
truck waiting, asked my mom to feed
his crew, fell asleep exhausted from
cleaning out the shop. I watched

his hands move in his sleep, his lips
fretting measurements. *It's OK,* my mother said,
just let your father work.

Blood History

My daughter sobs,
scared of the newness
rising from her eleven-year-old

body. I want to place
myself between her and the things
her uterus is about to do. I don't
say this. I say the scientific thing,
don't call it carnage coming. I call it

a blanket her body will build
for babies she doesn't have
to have. I know silence

can be a wreck—the way women
who raised my grandmother lodged
secrets behind their teeth so she

didn't know, at age fourteen
picking strawberries, why truth red
as that ran its finger down her
thigh. She thought she was dying.

My daughter's blood preparing.
My grandmother's blood,
bone dry. My own blood that first time
at the skating rink. My mother,

a pad and dismissal. The startle
of it still. I try to soften
it for myself too, say,
just bleeding, as though that's
a thing we can get used to.

What I Mean When I Say *Landscape*

The pond I broke
my arm on offers up
songs in a language

the color of my mother's
hair. If I knew I wouldn't
see you again, I would
say it—I want

to feel all your teeth
with my fingers, curl
my body into the ditch
under your tongue.

Have You Seen Instagram Lately?

I want to be one of those women
in WinCo with only a few things in her

cart: organic yogurt, flavored water, a small blue
orchid for the kitchen window. A quiet
Grace Kelly type, or at least Julianne Moore. I'd like

my mom jeans to lie real flat so I'm more
mannequin than mom. But where can I hide

my daughter, trailing behind, a prepubescent caboose
asking *Can I have this?* about a gummy food made to look
like a stackable burger, and I say *Yes*

to the gummy burger, perch it on the cereal
and toilet paper. She loves my legs—

draws them as trees in her notebook, her legs
tree trunks too, pine branches for our hair. She used to

grab the soft of my stomach or extra
under my arms when she sucked her thumb. The excess of me,

a comfort. A friend told me sex is the equivalent of
a seven-mile run, so I skipped the gym,

fucked a whole lot until I realized
if this were true, the world would be filled

with cigarette-slim legs, and Jesus! we'd be happy. But then how
could I stand with all these things

I carry: the church telling me marriage is God's
will, my father's crippled hands that don't look like

his hands, my son calling from the school auditorium
to say, *Mom, we're all so scared.*

A YouTube yogi tells me there's a thumbnail-sized
room at the back of my heart. He says it's where

my soul lives. I'd like to unzip
my skin, and bow-and-arrow myself
right in there, stretch out

on the couch. Are there flowers
or antlers on the mantel? Do I
have to split wood for the fire? Who
cleans the place up?

Meadowlark

What magic does a teenage boy use
to arrange his lips into perfect
birdsong? My brother

the only person who could
recreate the sweet trill we listened for
each spring. This bird in the waving
grass carrying my childhood in
a rise and fall of song I don't even know

how to whistle. How does a pasture of trees,
a pond of bluegill, a whole train track fit in
a brief, feathered body? My father

carried songs in him and rolled them
out for me on long drives. Old ballads
that made me know something
other kids my age didn't know. I still carry

them around with me, whisper
them in my children's rooms at night.
A meadowlark, tattooed
on my arm so I can't change

my mind about what I love. I lay still
for the pain and let that bird become
part of me. I would like to be a bird,
but without forgetting my father

or how walking through a field, my brother
put his hand out to stop me, said *Listen,* and we waited,
watching each other's face, for the music.

Your Dad Dies Today

First he eats bran flakes for breakfast
and you find a yogurt, barely expired
in the fridge. You ask if he'd like
to walk. You put *walk* in air quotes

because of the wheelchair.
He chooses a gravel road, embarrassed maybe
of his blue bathrobe and bare feet.

He says, *That fence*
is so straight. He says, *They must have*
hayed this field. He says, *Wouldn't it be nice*
to live here in the country but still
so close to town? He doesn't say,

I will die in eight hours.
or, *You will scream*
at your mother. He doesn't
say, *You will think of the CPR*
dummy in gym class when you breathe

your breath into me. And he doesn't
say, *It won't do*

any good. You don't walk far
before turning around. He checks
the empty mailbox, says he'd like to

lie down for a while. *Incredible,*
you say to your mom,
he must be feeling better.

The Mountain I Might Be

I've drawn my skin in
close to bone,
white-knuckled my breath
in lungs' deep hands,

carved round calves
with tiptoe steps,
dammed
my wildest rivers.

If I rip these words
from stomach walls
string them out
in the sun,

will they dry
fire
orange or soften
camas blue?

A bath with my daughter,
her hand on my spine.
Mama, she says,
You're a canyon.

A canyon, dark
water, a flicker's
fierce song breaking
the morning in two.

Rapture

Uncle Ron gives the sermon, explains

my father will be buried with his feet
East so on Resurrection Day
he will rise facing
Jerusalem. I try to keep

my crying quiet. I want to
sit with my disbelief—stay here
with the body. Instead I picture

a postcard circulated
through our Assembly of God

church. *The Rapture:* Jesus shining

in the sky. Below, cars crashing
into cars, airplanes exploding
against buildings and the left-behind

staring bewildered, at bodies floating
up from parking lots and roads—

the cemetery ground
cracked open. I lay

on my parents' bed and stared
into the eyes of this postcard Jesus, counting

backward from ten over and over
because I was so excited, and maybe
I couldn't wait.

Landlocked

The air above this man-made
reservoir turns violent
pink each afternoon. This is a tune

on a guitar I can barely
play. I've built
a forest of grief and you

aren't allowed in.
Fifteen miles from my childhood

home, water still waits
in Osage Pond. Carrots grow
in the garden my mother

abandoned, but the penny-sized frogs
have disappeared. My mind

reaches into my father's
coffin and finds just silence. I'm sure
that owl on the telephone
pole has nothing to do with me.
I used to dream

my father left me
by accident in our yellow canoe.
I'd wake to
the rhythm of waves

carrying me farther
and farther from shore.

My Middle School Boyfriend Comes to the Window

after the owls have started up and my kids are in bed.

You're forty now, he says.

I blush, ask, *How do I look?*

Not too bad, he says, and his voice cracks a little.

We were magic weren't we? I ask.

You gave me that Scottie Pippen poster, he says. *It's hanging in my locker.*

I gave you more than that, I say, *but you kissed Ashley anyway.*

She was sixteen, he says, *and so hot.*

I took off my pants for you, I say, *in Heather's basement.*

You smelled like the tanning bed, he says, *and I wasn't sure what to do.*

You go bald, I say, *I checked your Facebook.*

He runs his fingers through his thick brown hair.

Do you ever wonder? he asks.

Sometimes, I say. *When I hear the ball in my driveway hit the rim, I think of you kissing me after the game.*

You danced at halftime, he says, *I couldn't take my eyes off you, your tan arms circling the air again and again   like this.*

On Arriving

Each spring I brought
the first buttercup to my young
father, who paused stacking wood
or cleaning his shop to tuck it
behind his ear. I stretched

out my small legs and drifted
into every book I read. I stared
at the grain in wood, stared at the curves of boys'

shoulders, stared at the angels
who walked through my walls.
I saw seven of them

one winter morning and named them
all. I knew which words
held the curled-up voice
of God, but I still rode a bike
to the pool in my heart-

shaped glasses and sometimes wrecked blood
onto my knees. When trains
pushed through our pasture, I waved
at the engineer who'd wave back

at crumbling red dirt, white pine,
and sage brush
all dressed as a scab-kneed
girl in a worn-out, rainbow jumpsuit.

Five Days After the Funeral

I drank coffee with a spoonful of honey and my father's body was under the ground

I ran blisters onto my heels and my father's body was under the ground

I swept every bit of the front porch and my father's body was under the ground

I jumped into a mountain lake and the cold took my breath and my father's body was under the ground

I brushed my son's long black hair and my father's body was under the ground

I stood up too fast and the room went dark and my father's body was under the ground

My son asked if I was okay and my father's body was under the ground

I ordered extravagant razor clams and my father's body was under the ground

I put a five-dollar bill in a jukebox and played old country and my father's body was under the ground

I dreamed I asked my father a question as he rode a dark river toward the ocean but he didn't answer, just looked past me, eyes wide, reflecting the clouds

Country

Country girl, shake it for me. —Luke Bryan

I used to crouch in my dad's green Ford.
Rust on the sides made me feel

too country. Once a wolf crossed
our road, hunger pushing it beyond

familiar country. I kept my feelings for the neighbor
girl hidden in a cactus in the backcountry.

When my father could still walk, he danced
with my mom to Crystal Gayle—

healthy-years-love-song country. Our yard
was filled with starlings. Mom said

they don't belong in this country.
Our ex-mailman/preacher

swept his arms wide, said, *This*
is God's country. My father's body is

buried in cattle country. I filled my childhood
journal with red dirt, cactus flowers, white pines. I wanted

to write my country. My brother taught me
to sing the harmony, driving down

gravel country. I wore boots to school
once and my teacher said, *I didn't know*

you were country. The size of our pasture
broke my heart when I returned from

a different country. I've crowded
my shelves with winterkill, baby teeth, stones

painted to look like mountains. Don't tell me
that's not country.

Just After Breakfast

My ghost-dad rings
the doorbell, says he's been
antiquing. His seven arms

full of elk-ivory belt buckles,
Louis L'Amour novels,
candlesticks. I don't want to

close the door. I'd like to run

my fingers over the buckles,
read to him by candlelight,

but our dead shouldn't
bring so much
with them. Sometimes,

they're asking too much.

Storm Watch

Be careful out there.
Last night brought seven more
inches of snow, a flock of hungry

sparrows to the feeder,
and a painful lump
to the armpit side of my right
breast. Maybe

it's a fistful of grief
punching around or
a walnut-sized beehive.
Maybe a miniature city

complete with billboards and couples
kissing. I ask my husband
to feel it, and his hesitation
becomes a small suburb of pain.

Here's the doctor
now. Our sons play soccer
together, so we can talk about that

while he walks his fingers
all around my nipple. Did you know

you can wait two days
for a mammogram even
with a city buzzing inside?

And outside, the snow
piling up. You don't believe it
now, but one of these
days you'll notice
a tulip and look around to
find them everywhere.

What a Hawk Means

After a red-tailed hawk hit
our window, you could see
the mark of her wings.

My son and I ran to hold her
gaze where she sat stunned
on our small back porch.

She opened her beak
and my son's sixteen years
came spooling out
like measuring tape.

I noticed tucked in her feathers
the words he had just said,
Every day, I think of a new way
to die. The branches

above began to sing. I didn't
recognize the song, but it was
a reason to look away.

I Resurrect My Mother Who Isn't Actually Dead

And when she blooms her body back
into the air, she's starving,
so she eats all her *I'm sorrys*.
She picks up her childhood

self, stuffs cotton in her ears
when her Pentecostal father jokes
girls are good for cookin', lovin', and babies.
My resurrected mother two-steps

through her forties, past her twenties, straight
into nineteen where she whispers, *I don't,*
to the young man asking,
Do you? My resurrected mother

is allowed to paint her nails coral,
see Frankie and Annette on the screen,
wear the canary-yellow pants
she admires in a window.

I resurrect my mother into not-a-mother
and this complicates things for me, but for now
I'm holding it in my hands

like a snow globe. I turn it over, shake it
hard. I pass it around and say, *See that*
woman in high-waisted pants brushing her bangs
from her eyes—her bright fingertips
shining? Isn't she something?

What Were We Hoping For?

My ghost-dad takes over
the old recliner, moves

my cat to the floor. God,
he looks young. My brother

stares, and I know
he's thinking it too. My

ghost-dad bends
over my sleeping son,

smells his black curls.
He's embroidered

words onto all our clothes,
baked twenty-two

loaves of bread. There's no more
room on the counter.

He's opening
and closing the curtains.

My brother cups his hands
around his mouth, whispers in

my direction, *This*
isn't fun anymore.

Given

Here are dark eye circles dressed

as country ponds, a coffeepot dripping

expectations, and blue aphids sparkling

in the knots of your hair. Here is a PowerPoint

presentation on whether men find your body

acceptable. A fistfight in your kitchen,

a fruit basket of the last twenty years, and a yoga pose

guaranteed to make you cry. Here is a drunk-text

and a list of tasks you can complete

while grieving. Here is a coffee shop called *Don't Think*

about Dying. Here, you aren't allowed to

say to your father. Here are his enduring fingernails.

Here is the person you thought you'd be

by forty curled inside an orange peel.

Here is a horse eating grass

growing up from a buried dog and

a vase of moth wings pretending

to be flowers.

Homage to My Being a Woman

In the pink light of morning all my grandmothers
come in vagaries and spring hats, dead
eyes shining. They keep me
awake with gossip, walk through
shower spray, rattle their teeth
in drinking glasses. Some evenings

they quiet like warm ash
in my woodstove, burn
just below the surface. Some evenings
they flicker light bulbs, squeeze the cheeks
of my sleeping children, scream
tea kettle warnings. Their fingers are

carrot flowers. When they
brush my hands, I cry.
I push their dirt back into soil,

but they squeeze into
my silence. Their songs
become sorrow
songs. They remember

their children. They dance a bare-legged dance
to the alley and back, tear pages
from books, anchor themselves to the walls
with names I don't know. They speak

in tongues, nap on my couch, snore notes
I heard once when the only circus that ever came
to my town came. When a woman in ripped tights

rode an aging elephant through the tent.
They roll their stories
in zigzags, pass them around.
They say, *I insist.*

My grandmothers' voices cling
to the ceiling, drip
onto our plates, curdle our milk.

They click into our dreams, rub their wings
together. They pull at my stomach skin,

my breasts, smooth the wrinkles of my mouth,
read the cards of my regrets. They give us gifts:
dead beetles, owl pellets, skulls of baby
birds. They have wrapped them in
trembling. They are at home in trembling.

My grandmothers are turkey feathers and songs
we protect like recipes, like star quilts.
It's all I've really wanted—

their clothes on old wire lines, western wind
in their faces. All of our fingers, reaching
for each other, for other witch
hazel women.

In my fortieth year, I'm still asking
for a sign, a ring in my coffee,
a bee on my pillow. Who can call forth

my grandmothers? Who can beg them
to stay? They have painted my rooms

with an itching, a sandpaper
moan. I am trying to give them
my children, my abandoned
childhood poems. I cannot help
but sit among them.

I brush their obsidian hair.
I oil their brittle bones.

ACKNOWLEDGMENTS

Thank you to these journals who published the following poems, though some have since been changed.

About Place Journal: Dignity as an Endangered Species in the 21st Century "Have You Seen Instagram Lately?"
The American Journal of Poetry "The Sign on the Highway Reads, 'Best Town on Earth'"
Bellingham Review "It Was the Summer of Hard Tomatoes"
Blood Orange Review "Church," "An Altar in the World," "In the Tree Fort"
Copper Nickel "After Dark," "God Was Always Talking"
Driftwood Press "The Mountain I Might Be"
Etched Onyx Magazine, "I Build an Altar for My Family to Pray," "Playground," "Hypothetical," "We Were Mothers"
The Examined Life Journal "Is This What the Yeti Feels?"
Frontier Poetry "Boil Down"
High Desert Journal "Andi and Me, by Bighorn Creek"
Mary Journal "Thoughts from My Time on the Moon"
The Meadow "Creation Myth of My Father"
Mid-American Review "Homage to My Being a Woman"
Northwest Review "There Now"
Terrain.org "Miscarriage," "Mother, Any Given Day," "For Cousins"
San Pedro River Review "On Arriving"
Up North Lit "Given"
Zócalo Public Square "Landlocked"

THANK YOU

Thank you to the teachers and professors who taught me and encouraged me, especially Kent Meyers, Vincent King, Joy Passanante, Robert Wrigley, Alexandra Teague, Michael McGriff, and Brian Blanchfield.

Thank you to my cohort at the University of Idaho MFA program who workshopped several of these poems and whose work inspired me in so many ways. With a special thanks to Dylan Gould, CMarie Fuhrman, Josh Hamilton, Canese Jarboe, and Cameron McGill. And with a heart full of love and gratitude to my writing bestie and tiny life coach, Samantha Burns.

Thank you to Taylor Ranch, Elk River Writer's Conference, and Winter Tangerine. Thank you Cass Cleghorn.

Thank you to my children and best adventure Noah, Juan, and Ruby. To Brant Miller. To my mother and siblings. And to Tyler Palmer.

And a special thanks to my father who bought me books of poetry to read out loud to him and asked occasionally for the folder where I kept my poetry so he could sit and read through it all.

ABOUT STACY BOE MILLER

Stacy Boe Miller is a prose writer and a poet. She graduated with an MFA in Creative Writing from the University of Idaho in 2019. Some of her honors and awards include a Writing in the Wild Fellowship, Winter Tangerine Fellowship, Terrain Editor's Prize, and three years serving as Poet Laureate of Moscow, Idaho, where she still teaches community writing workshops. Her work can be found in *The Sun, Copper Nickel, Mid-American Review, Bellingham Review, Terrain.org,* and other journals. More of her work, including information about the *WorkWhile* podcast, can be found at stacyboemiller.com.

www.ingramcontent.com/pod-product-compliance
Lightning Source LLC
LaVergne TN
LVHW051020080826
845145LV00009B/2717

* 9 7 8 1 9 4 9 5 4 0 6 0 4 *